The
World's
YUCKIEST
joke book!

Books by John Byrne
CRAZY CLASSROOM JOKE BOOK
THE ULTIMATE JOKE HANDBOOK
THE WORLD'S DEADLIEST JOKE BOOK
THE WORLD'S SCARIEST JOKE BOOK
THE WORLD'S YUCKIEST JOKE BOOK

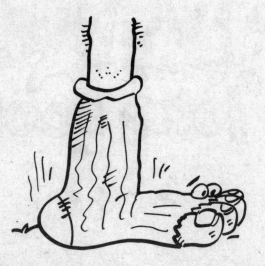

John Byrne is a cartoonist, comedy writer and agony uncle for the *Stage* newspaper. Of course if you've read any of his other joke books you'll know all about agony. We would like to point out that he has none of the bad habits featured in this book. (And yes, we have told him lying is a VERY bad habit!)

The World's YUCKIEST joke book!

John Byrne

PUFFIN

For Paul Lamb – one of the least yucky people I know

PUFFIN BOOKS

Published by the Penguin Group
Penguin Books Ltd, 80 Strand, London WC2R 0RL, England
Penguin Group (USA), Inc., 375 Hudson Street, New York, New York 10014, USA
Penguin Books Australia Ltd, 250 Camberwell Road, Camberwell, Victoria 3124, Australia
Penguin Books Canada Ltd, 10 Alcorn Avenue, Toronto, Ontario, Canada M4V 3B2
Penguin Books India (P) Ltd, 11 Community Centre, Panchsheel Park, New Delhi – 110 017, India
Penguin Group (NZ), cnr Airborne and Rosedale Roads, Albany, Auckland 1310, New Zealand
Penguin Books (South Africa) (Pty) Ltd, 24 Sturdee Avenue, Rosebank 2196, South Africa

Penguin Books Ltd, Registered Offices: 80 Strand, London WC2R 0RL, England

www.penguin.com

First published 2004
1

The moral right of the author/illustrator has been asserted

Made and printed in England by Clays Ltd, St Ives plc

British Library Cataloguing in Publication Data
A CIP catalogue record for this book is available from the British Library

ISBN 0–141–31360–9

PONGRATULATIONS!

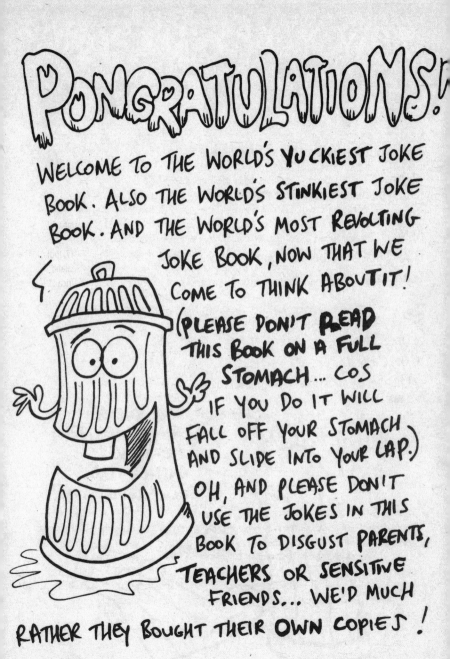

WELCOME TO THE WORLD'S YUCKIEST JOKE BOOK. ALSO THE WORLD'S STINKIEST JOKE BOOK. AND THE WORLD'S MOST REVOLTING JOKE BOOK, NOW THAT WE COME TO THINK ABOUT IT!

(PLEASE DON'T READ THIS BOOK ON A FULL STOMACH... COS IF YOU DO IT WILL FALL OFF YOUR STOMACH AND SLIDE INTO YOUR LAP.)

OH, AND PLEASE DON'T USE THE JOKES IN THIS BOOK TO DISGUST PARENTS, TEACHERS OR SENSITIVE FRIENDS... WE'D MUCH RATHER THEY BOUGHT THEIR OWN COPIES!

HOW YUCKY ARE YOU?

Test yourself with this queasy quiz.

1. Do you belch loudly after every meal?
a) Yes.
b) No.
c) You'll have to repeat the question. I was belching too loudly to hear it.

2. How often do you change your socks?
a) Once a week.
b) Once a year.
c) Change my socks? Now there's an idea.

ARE THERE ANY CLUES TO HELP ME ANSWER THE 'SOCK' QUESTION?

CHECK THE FOOTNOTES!

WHIFF!

3. Do your armpits smell?
a) Yes.
b) No.
c) Actually I use my nose to smell with, like everyone else.

4. Do you break wind in lifts?
a) Yes.
b) No.
c) Since I started breaking wind, nobody gives me lifts any more.

LIFT
GOING UP ○
GOING DOWN ○
GOING 'PARP!' ○

BIG CLOUD OF YUCKI-NESS!

5. Is your bedroom messy?
a) Yes.
b) No.
c) Can you send me a new copy of the quiz, please? I lost the first one somewhere in my bedroom.

6. How often do you clean your teeth?
a) Daily.
b) Weekly.
c) Whenever I can find the jar they're in.
(I TOLD you my room was messy!)

GREAT! I LOVE JOKES ABOUT STINKY DENTURES!

YEAH! THEY CHEER ME UP WHEN I'M DOWN IN THE MOUTH!

7. Do you have terrible table manners?
a) Yes.
b) No.
c) Compared to MY manners, my table is
very well behaved indeed.

8. Do you show a complete lack of respect?
a) Yes.
b) No.
c) Get lost and stop asking me stupid
questions!

What your answers mean:
Forget it! With the state of the paper you handed in, our examiner
refused to touch it with a ten-foot pole.

starting at the
bottom

Why did the toilet paper roll
down the hill?
Because it wanted to get to the bottom.

Did you hear about the Indian
chief who drank fifteen cups
of tea before bed?
He drowned in his tea-pee.

Why was the sand wet?
Because the sea-weed.
(Submitted by Seth.)

Why did the boy bring toilet paper to the birthday party? Because he was a party pooper.

If you go into the bathroom British and come out American, what are you while you're in the bathroom? Eur-o-pe-an. (You're-a-peein'.)

Do you know anyone who's been on the telly?
Only my sister. She uses the potty now.

What did Mr Spock see in the toilet?
The Captain's log.

YUK! GOOD MANNERS SEEM TO BE ALIEN IN THIS BOOK!

OH NO! WE'RE ONLY ON PAGE NINE AND ALREADY THERE'S A BEAR BOTTOM!

What is the first lesson baby polar bears receive from their mums? 'Don't eat the yellow snow.'

What's brown and on a diet? Skinny the Poo.

What vegetable do you never want to find in your toilet? A leek.

SORRY!
THIS PAGE HAS BEEN COVERED UP AS THE PICTURE IT CONTAINS IS
TOO YUCKY EVEN
FOR A BOOK LIKE THIS!
SIGNED THE EDITOR
THAT'S A BIT STRANGE ISN'T IT?
YES- NORMALLY THE AUTHOR PHOTO IS ON THE BACK COVER!

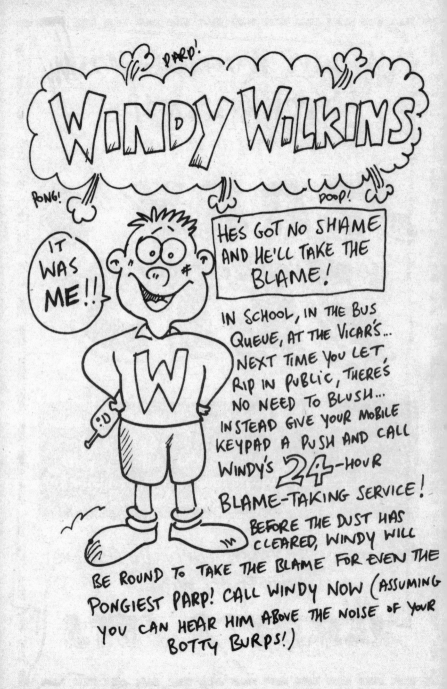

Windy? Worried? Wish you weren't?

Now you can rely on...

JERRY'S JETS

Remember: If You're Farty, Do Not Fret, Pass It Off With

JERRY'S JETS

Turn your 'Silent But Deadly' into 'Silent But Delicious' with

Farty Fragrances

Simply take one of these tablets in the morning, and throughout the day your botty burps will be fragranced with the most delicate and pleasant aromas. Why have your gusts of wind greeted with disgust when they can be greeted with cheers and thank yous instead?

AH! PHEW-TIFUL!

Fragrances available

Pot Pourri

Strawberry

Aroma Free *

* Mainly because we send you no tablets and nick your money.

FARTY PARTY

Where do farts go
on holiday?
Hong Pong.

Where do farts
wash dishes?
In the stink.

Who farts all the time and never grows up?
Peter Pong.

Who was Peter Pong's best friend?
Windy.

What is invisible and smells like a banana?
A monkey's fart.

Did you hear the joke about the fart?
You don't want to, it stinks.

YUK IDOLS

WHO WILL BE TOP OF THE PLOPS?

NO 1: DAN DRUFF

FAVOURITE FOOD: ICE CREAM (WITH FLAKE)

FAVOURITE SONG: 'THERE'S NO BUSINESS LIKE SNOW BUSINESS'

FAVOURITE SINGER: I DON'T LIKE SINGERS, I LIKE DEEJAYS — ESPECIALLY ONES THAT SCRATCH.

THE QUEEN OF HEARTS WAS BAKING

ON A SUMMER'S DAY,
WHEN ALL AT ONCE SHE SMELLED
A SMELL THAT MADE HER RUN AWAY.
THE KNAVE OF HEARTS WAS RUNNING
   TO THE TOILET IN A HURRY...

LITTLE MISS MUFFET SAT ON
    HER TUFFET
EATING HER CURDS AND WHEY.
ALONG CAME A SPIDER AND
    SAT DOWN BESIDE HER ...
BUT HE SHOULD HAVE JUMPED
OUT OF THE WAY!

URP!

YUKKY .. SMELLY BURP!

SORRY...CURDS ALWAYS UPSET MY STOMACH!

LITTLE BOY BLUE,
COME BLOW ON YOUR HORN,
THERE ARE SHEEP IN THE MEADOW
AND COWS IN THE CORN.
WHERE IS THE BOY WHO WAS
MINDING THE SHEEP?
HE FELL IN A COWPAT
SIX FEET DEEP!

HUMPTY DUMPTY SAT ON THE WALL.
HUMPTY DUMPTY HAD A
GREAT FALL.
ALL THE KING'S HORSES AND
ALL THE KING'S MEN
SAID

PEEYOOO!
WHAT WAS HUMPTY'S
'SELL BY' DATE
AGAIN?

M ARY HAD A LITTLE LAMB
    IT'S FLEECE WAS WHITE AS SNOW,
AND EVERYWHERE THAT MARY WENT
  THE LAMB WAS SURE TO 'GO'.

IT FOLLOWED HER TO SCHOOL ONE DAY,
WHICH WAS AGAINST THE RULE,
THAT'S WHY AROUND THE TEACHER'S
  DESK
THERE'S A GREAT BIG YELLOW POOL!

DEAD FUNNY

What do you call a guy who was born in
Australia, married in India and died in Russia?
Dead.

What is Beethoven doing in his grave?
Decomposing.

R.I.P.

HOPE YOU LIKE
ALL THESE 'GRAVE'
JOKES... I KNOW
SOME PEOPLE
JUST DON'T
DIG THEM!

WHAT'S A SKELETON'S FAVOURITE DINNER?

BONES IN GRAVE-Y

What do you get if you cross a budgie with a lawnmower?
Shredded tweet.

What happened to the fly that got trapped in a hairdresser's window?
Nothing. He just curled up and dyed.

Why are graveyards always so noisy?
Because of all the coffin.

WHY DID NOBODY HEAR THE SPOOK'S BOTTY BURPS?

NASTY

GHOSTLY

GUFF

BECAUSE HE WAITED TILL THE GHOST WAS CLEAR!

My friend used to be a magician's assistant who was sawn in half every night.
She had to leave because she just wasn't cut out for the job.

YUK IDOLS

WHO WILL BE TOP OF THE PLOPS?

NO 2: THE BOGIE BOYS

FAVOURITE FOOD: PICK 'N' MIX

FAVOURITE SONG: 'THERE'S NOSE BUSINESS LIKE SHOW BUSINESS'

FAVOURITE SINGER: NONE - IN FACT WE LOOK DOWN OUR NOSE AT THE COMPETITION.

Is your family

EMBARRASSED

by your bad habits?

NOSE PICKING? BURPING? STINKY SOCKS? TERRIBLE BREATH?

This is a job for

HYPNO HARRY

Just one session with me and your family will never be embarrassed by your bad habits again.

(Chiefly because during that one session I'll move into your house, and if they think YOUR bad habits are embarrassing, I guarantee you mine are even worse!)

GROSS!

Who likes nasty things better, a frog
or the son of a supermarket owner?
The son — he's a little grocer.

Sister: Why did you put a worm
in my bed?
Brother: Because you would
have been able to see a snake
under the covers.

I'M SUPPOSED TO
SHED MY SKIN... BUT
EVERY TIME I GO INTO
THE SHED, PEOPLE RUN
OUT SCREAMING!

Sister: What's the difference
between pepperoni and a cowpat?
Brother: I don't know.
Sister: Obviously not the taste if you
enjoyed that pizza I made you.

Barry: When my big brother's zits pop,
it's disgusting.
Larry: Oh, be fair, lots of teenagers have
zits that pop.
Barry: Yes, but he makes me pop them!

WHAT DO YOU WRITE ON A GREETINGS CARD WITH INDIGESTION?

HAPPY BURP-DAY!

URRRP!

Brother: Come quick! The bath plug hole is clogged up with Dad's hairs.
Sister: So what?
Brother: They're still attached to his head.

Sister: Guess what you're getting for your birthday?
Brother: What?
Sister: Bad breath and B.O., same as you get every other day of the year.

WARNING!

FOR ALL OF YOU WHO THINK THIS YUCKY JOKE BOOK CAN'T LIVE UP TO ITS TITLE...

THE NEXT PAGE CONTAINS A PICTURE THAT'S ABSOLUTELY

STOMACH TURNING!

YES- BUT SINCE THEY GAVE US THESE NEW SWITCHES THAT TURN OUR STOMACHS ON AND OFF, IT'S BEEN SO MUCH EASIER!
CLICK!
OFF

THIS IS FUNNY...NO, IT'S SNOT!

WHAT DOES A GIANT GORILLA USE TO WIPE HIS NOSE?

ER... ANYONE WHO HAPPENS TO BE PASSING?

Why does a gorilla have big nostrils? Because it has big fingers.

What is the difference between bogies and broccoli? Kids don't eat broccoli.

What old English tune is like a boy with no hankie? 'Greensleeves'.

What do you call a monster that picks his nose?
The Bogie Man.

AT LEAST PINOCCHIO'S GOT ENOUGH MANNERS NOT TO PICK HIS NOSE...

IT'S NOT BECAUSE HE'S GOT MANNERS... IT'S COS HE HASN'T GOT LONG ENOUGH ARMS!

Why did the stupid boy take his nose apart?
He wanted to see what made it run.

YUK IDOLS

WHO WILL BE TOP OF THE PLOPS?

No 3: SAL LYVA

FAVOURITE FOOD: TONGUE

FAVOURITE SONG: 'SLURPERCALI-
FRAGILISTIC-
EXPIALIDOCIOUS'
(IT'S QUITE A MOUTHFUL!)

FAVOURITE SINGER: NONE — I CAN
LICK THEM ALL!

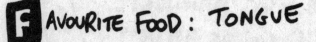

Worried about making an impression?

Don't enter a room without using some of our patented

UNDERARM SPRAY

We guarantee it will get you noticed!*

***Mostly because our spray will make everything it touches smell like your underarms. Try it for yourself. We're sure you'll agree that life without it is just the pits.**

SICK STUFF

What floats on water
and has carrots in?
Sea sick.

I'M GETTING REALLY BORED... I'VE BEEN HANGING AROUND THE AIRPORT FOR AGES, AND NONE OF THE PLANES HAVE FELT SICK YET.

AIR SICKNESS BAG

Why are there always bits of carrot in vomit? Because if there were whole carrots, they'd get stuck in your throat.

What's the world's sickest animated movie? *Wallis and Vomit.*

What did one piece of
digested carrot say to the
other piece?
'Do you want to go out with
me?'

Why was the vomit sad?
It was just a poor retch.

Who lives in a tee-pee
and feels sick?
Puke-a-hontas.

YUK IDOLS

WHO WILL BE TOP OF THE PLOPS?

PARP!

NO 4: BOTT E. BURP

FAVOURITE FOOD : BEANS, OF COURSE

FAVOURITE SONG: 'THERE'S NO BUSINESS LIKE BLOW BUSINESS'

FAVOURITE SINGER: IF YOU ASK ME, THEY ALL STINK!

BLOOD, BOILS AND BLISTERS

'Teacher, teacher, I think I'm built
upside down!'
'What makes you say that?'
'Well, my nose runs and my feet smell!'

HOW DO YOU
TRAIN A
PIMPLE?

TEACH
IT TO
'ZIT'!

'Doctor, Doctor, will this cream
cure my acne?'
'I never make rash promises.'

What's small and mischievous
and covered in blood?
A haemo-goblin.

What did one blood vessel say
to the other blood vessel?
'Stop being such a clot!'

What do you call a
conceited blood vessel?
Vein.

What do you say when you cut
your finger on the newspaper?
'Bleed all about it.'

Why aren't there more newspapers
for blood vessels to read?
They wouldn't have much circulation.

WHAT DO YOU CALL
IT WHEN YOUR BOILS
KEEP MOANING AT
YOU?

A
'SKIN
COMPLAINT'

What's a pimple's favourite
sport?
Basketboil.

What do you say to a pimple on
his birthday?
'For squeeze a jolly good fellow.'

What do you call a dog that's
covered in pimples?
Spot.

WHAT DO YOU
GIVE A BOIL WITH
A HEADACHE?

A PIM-PILL!

MIRROR, MIRROR, ON THE WALL, WHO'S THE PIMPLIEST ONE OF ALL?

What do you call a cat that's covered in pimples?
Pus.

What do you call a pimple that eats other pimples?
A canni-boil.

What did the pimple say to the nose?
'I haven't spotted you in a long time.'

IT MUST BE YOU, SO UPON REFLECTION- PLEASE STOP LOOKING IN MY DIRECTION!

How do you start a pimple race?
From scratch.

What's big, red and dangerous and carries a whip?
Indiana Jones and the Pimple of Doom.

Where do pimples hide at school?
Behind the boil-cycle sheds.

Do your friends complain about your bad breath? Switch to

BRUSHO

toothpaste

— and see the difference.

You'll still have terrible breath but after you've filled your ears with toothpaste, you won't hear your friends complaining any more.

Wipe that frown off your face with

POWER PIMPLE CREAM

If you find that ordinary pimple creams don't work for you, try the most powerful product on the market. Just one dab and we guarantee that every blemish will disappear from your face!*

*Mainly because your face will disintegrate. But don't worry. You can use the leftover power pimple cream for cleaning old engine parts or as a lethal weedkiller.

GRUNGE

URRGH! YOU'RE THE PONGIEST PANTS I'VE EVER SMELT... HAVEN'T YOU GOT ANY SOAP POWDER?

I DID HAVE... BUT IT GOT 'KNICK'ED!

I wear fresh socks every day. By Sunday, I can't get my shoes on.

My underpants are completely insane. They are pantaloons.

Why did Big Ears
buy deodorant?
To hide his Noddy
odour.

Where do you put underpants
that haven't been washed for
three weeks?
Anywhere you like – they'll still be
able to move all by themselves.

I WOULDN'T
GO TO THE OPPOSITE
PAGE IF I WERE
YOU...THAT
MONK IS COVERED
IN GREASE!

Is it hard to learn to fart softly?
No, it's a breeze.

Why did the heavy-metal fan
put a carpet on his head?
He wanted his hair to be matted.

WELL, OF COURSE I'M COVERED IN GREASE... I'M A FRIAR!

Heard about the monastery where
the laundry broke down?
The monks all had disgusting habits.

Who runs through the town and
pees on all the lampposts?
Wee Willie Winkie.

YUK IDOLS

WHO WILL BE TOP OF THE PLOPS?

NO 5:
E.R. WAX

Favourite FOOD : HERRING (BECAUSE I LIKE HERRING AIDS)

Favourite SONG : 'EAR WE GO, EAR WE GO, EAR WE GO'

Favourite SINGER : DON'T ASK ME — THEY ALL SOUND THE SAME TO ME.

Dissed in the dressing room? Poked fun at on the pitch?

Yes, there's nothing more embarrassing than turning up to start a new sport and having everyone know you're a beginner from your brand new clean clothes. It's time you ordered a pair of

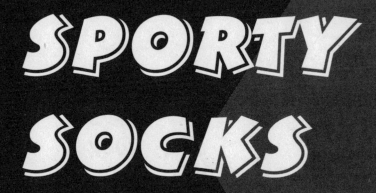

SPORTY SOCKS

– the socks with the whiff of experience.

Every pair of Sporty Socks is guaranteed to have been pre-worn by at least seven sweaty rugby players. Take them out of your kit bag and we promise nobody will ever laugh at you again!*

*Mainly because they smell so bad you'll have the whole dressing room to yourself!)

On the Menu

What happened when the chef found a
daddy long legs in the salad?
It became a daddy short legs.

What is red and dangerous?
Strawberry and tarantula jam.

What do you get if you cross cockroaches
with peanut butter?
Extra-crunchy peanut butter.

How do we know that insects are clever?
Because they always know when you are
having a picnic.

KNEES, KNEES, KNEES, KNEES, KNEES

What do you get if you cross a centipede
with a chicken?
Enough drumsticks to feed an army.

What is the difference between school dinners
and a pile of slugs?
School dinners come on a plate.

'I had to eat yeast and shoe polish for breakfast.'
'Why?'
'Because my mum wanted me to rise and shine every morning.'

What's the difference between
maggots and worms?
Maggots are more crunchy.

What's the difference between a
worm and an apple?
Have you ever tried worm pie?

What's worse than finding a maggot
in your apple?
Finding half a maggot.

Why did the girl eat the glow worm?
She wanted a light meal.

YECCH! WITH JOKES
LIKE THAT, THERE'S NOT
MUCH CHANCE OF US
WORMING OUR WAY INTO
YOUR AFFECTIONS!

Why do worms taste like chewing gum?
Because they're Wrigleys.

HOW BAD ARE YOUR MANNERS?

1. Bad Manners are . . . eating with your fingers.

   Really Bad Manners are . . . eating someone else's fingers.

2. Bad Manners are . . . talking with your mouth full.

   Really Bad Manners are . . . singing with your mouth full.

...Manners are ... leaving the
...t seat up.

...y Bad Manners are ... blowing
...toilet seat up.

...Manners are ... leaving a ring
...d the bath.

...ly Bad Manners are ... wearing
...bath like a ring.

'SPECIALLY
IF YOU DON'T
CLEAN THE
DIRTY WATER
OUT FIRST!

5. Bad Manners are ... using bad language.

Really Bad Manners are ... using bad language and ventriloquism.

6. Bad Manners are ... playing with your food.

Really Bad Manners are ... playing with your food after you've eaten it.

7. Bad Manners are ... reading over somebody's shoulder.

Really Bad Manners are ... making somebody read this book over YOUR shoulder.

... OF COURSE, WHEN THEY'RE SICK ON YOUR HEAD, YOU'LL REGRET IT!

DO SCHOOL DINNERS GIVE YOU INDIGESTION?

FIGHT BACK WITH

DIGESTO
TABLETS

JUST ONE TABLET IS GUARANTEED TO SOLVE THE PROBLEM!

(BECAUSE EACH TABLET IS A METRE IN DIAMETER AND WEIGHS FIVE TONNES. SIMPLY ROLL IT IN FRONT OF THE KITCHEN DOOR AND THE DINNER LADIES WON'T BE ABLE TO GET OUT.)

WHO WILL BE TOP OF THE PLOPS?

NO 6: STINK E. SOCK

F AVOURITE FOOD: SOLE

F AVOURITE SONG: 'THERE'S NO BUSINESS LIKE TOE BUSINESS'

F AVOURITE SINGER: I PREFER COMEDIANS. THEY HAVE ME IN STITCHES!

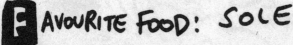

Creepy Crawlies

What do you call an ant
with five pairs of eyes?
Ant-ten-eye.

What games do elephants
play with ants?
Squash.

What do you call a very
smelly ant?
De-odour-ant.

WHEN YOU'VE GOT AS MANY ARMPITS AS I, YOU DO NEED A LOT OF ANT-1-PERSPIRANT!

HEY! WANNA HEAR SOME YUCKY STORIES?

SORRY, SPIDER... MUST FLY...

Why don't anteaters
get sick?
Because they are
full of ant-i-bodies.

What do you get if you cross
some ants with some ticks?
All sorts of antics.

What's the definition
of a caterpillar?
A hairy worm.

What is worse than an alligator
with toothache?
A centipede with athlete's foot.

What has fifty legs but
can't walk?
Half a centipede.

What do you call a
rabbit with fleas?
Bugs Bunny.

WHY ARE YOU LOT HOUNDING ME WITH THESE AWFUL FLEA JOKES?

What is the difference
between a flea and a wolf?
One prowls on the hairy and
the other howls on the prairie.

How do you find where
a flea has bitten you?
You start from scratch.

What is the difference
between fleas and dogs?
Dogs can have fleas but
fleas can't have dogs.

WE TRIED NOT
TO...

... BUT AS SOON
AS WE JUMPED
ON YOUR BACK WE
GOT CARRIED
AWAY!

How do fleas travel?
They itch-hike.

What is the most faithful insect?
A flea. Once they find someone
they like, they stick to them.

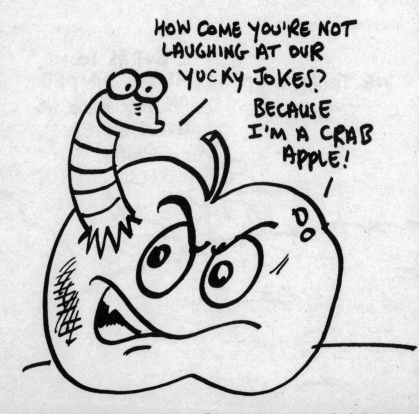

HOW COME YOU'RE NOT LAUGHING AT OUR YUCKY JOKES?

BECAUSE I'M A CRAB APPLE!

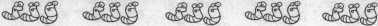

What did one flea say to
the other after a night out?
'Shall we walk home or
take a dog?'

What is a mosquito's
favourite sport?
Skin-diving.

What has antlers and
sucks blood?
A moose-quito.

Two fleas running across a cereal packet.
One says to the other, 'Why are we running
so fast?'
'Because it says, "Tear along the dotted line"!'

What did the maggot say to his friend
when he got stuck in an apple?
'Worm your way out of that one!'

Why didn't the two worms get on
Noah's Ark in an apple?
Because everyone had to go in pears.

HI, I'M A HUGE DISGUSTING BUNNY-EATING MONSTER.

'Doctor, Doctor, I keep dreaming that there are huge insects playing Scrabble under my bed. What should I do?'
'Hide the scrabble board.'

What's yellow, wiggles and is dangerous?
A maggot with attitude.

Own a snake?
A rat?
A cockroach?

If you've got a more disgusting – er – interesting type of pet, you'll know how difficult it is to find a pet-sitter for it. Not any more! Simply book a pet-sitter from

PETRIFYING PETS, INC.

And you can go on holiday with complete peace of mind. Our pet-sitters are guaranteed not to be afraid of even the scariest, most horrible pet.*

*Mainly because our pet-sitters are all giant mutant lizards and more disgusting than any pet they may be asked to look after. Don't try asking for your money back either – our banker is also a giant mutant lizard.

YUK IDOLS

WHO WILL BE TOP OF THE PLOPS?

NO 7: PLOPPY WILLIAMS

FAVOURITE FOOD: CREAM BUMS

FAVOURITE SONG: NO FAVOURITES – ALL MY SONGS ONLY GET TO 'NUMBER TWO'.

FAVOURITE SINGER: PAVOR-BOTTI

Ask Auntie Septic

Embarrassing personal questions will get instant understanding.*

* You'll understand instantly that you've mentioned them to the wrong person.

Dear Auntie
I have a terrible habit of breaking wind in lifts. What can I do about this?
Windy, Woking

Dear Windy
Take the stairs.

URGH! THAT JOKE IS NEAR THE KNUCKLE!

Dear Auntie
How can I stop biting my fingernails?
Chewy, Chippenham

Dear Chewy
Hire someone else to bite them for you.

Dear Auntie
How can I stop talking with my mouth full?
Hungry, Hampton

Dear Hungry
Sorry can't speak at the moment – I'm busy biting Chewy of Chippenham's fingernails.

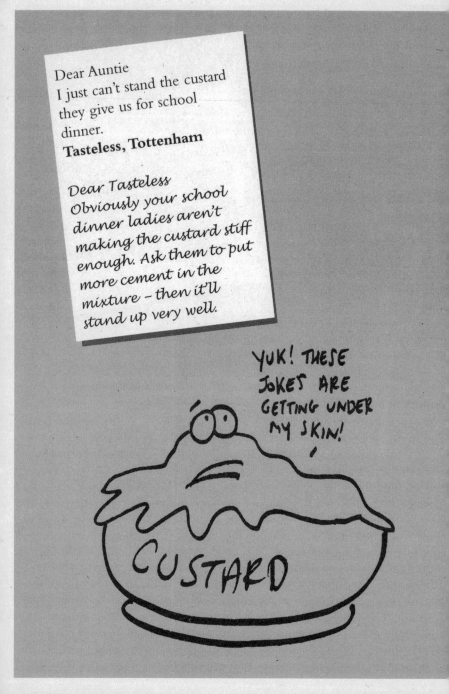

SOME OF THESE TOOTH PUNS ARE SO BAD THEY DESERVE A PLAQUE!

Dear Auntie
My teeth are very bad. Should I have them taken out?
Molars, Merton

Dear Molars
Certainly not! If your teeth are bad, they certainly don't deserve to be rewarded with a trip to the cinema or a restaurant.

Dear Auntie
I seem to have picked up a really yucky, highly contagious disease – what do you think I should do?
Spotty, Stockwell

Dear Spotty
You should take your letter back, quick, in case I catch something from it!

I DON'T KNOW WHY
EVERYONE'S COMPLAINING...
WE SMELLY OLD SOCKS
LI<u>KE</u> CORNY JOKES...

Dear Auntie
Are you sure it's safe to tell you about my embarrassing personal problems? I'd hate anyone else to find out about them.
Shy, Shadwell

Dear Shy
Of course it's safe to tell me about your embarrassing personal problems. All letters to me are completely confidential. And after I showed yours to your parents, your teachers and everyone in your school, they all agreed you were right to want to keep it to yourself.

Dear Auntie
Every time I see an old sock I have to pick it up and eat it. Is that disgusting?
Peckish, Peckham

Dear Peckish
It certainly is. Haven't you ever learned to eat your socks with a knife and fork?

...MIND YOU, WE ALSO LIKE BUNION-Y JOKES, ATHLETE'S FOOT-Y JOKES, VERRUCA-Y JOKES...

YUK IDOLS

WHO WILL BE TOP OF THE PLOPS?

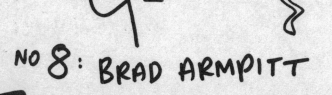

NO 8: BRAD ARMPITT

Favourite FOOD : SAUSAGE ROLL-ONS

Favourite SONG : 'THERE'S NO BUSINESS LIKE B.O. BUSINESS'

Favourite SINGER: ANYONE WHO WORKS UP A SWEAT!

   86

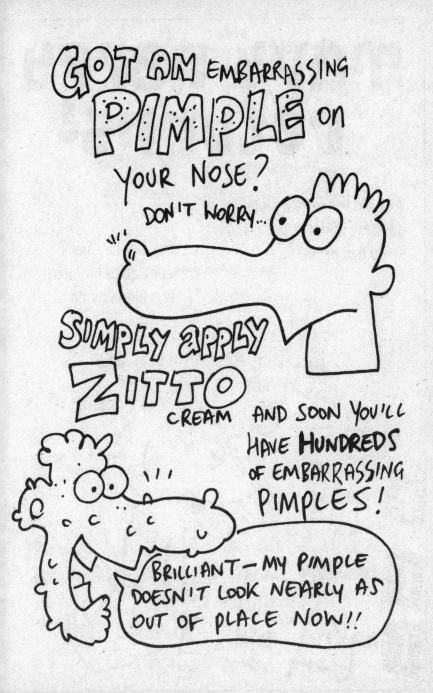

many nappy returns!

Why did the smelly nappy
go home from the nursery?
It had had its fill.

Why did the smelly
nappy go to hospital?
For a plop-eration.

ROSES ARE RED, VIOLETS ARE
BLUE... HURRY UP, MUM - I'VE
JUST DONE
A
POO!

HAPPY MOTHER'S DAY

Why did the car have smelly
nappies across the front
window?
They were windscreen diapers.

What did one smelly nappy say
to the other smelly nappy?
'Just who do you stink you are?'

What do you call a
boastful smelly nappy?
Full of himself.

Why don't smelly nappies like
toilet training?
Because it drives them potty.

What's a smelly nappy's
favourite dessert?
Whiffed cream.

'I need to go and change a nappy for
my little brother.'
'I didn't know you could do swaps.'

World's Yuckiest

BAD BREATH by Hal E. Tosis

BLOOD AND GUTS BY N. TESTINES

NO TOILET PAPER by I. M. Provise

How to Avoid Washing by B.O. Constantly

STAINED SHIRTS by Tom Atto-Sauce

GERMAN GROOMING MISTAKES BY HERR UPYERNOSE

Bookshelf

A Guide to Farting by Wyn D. Pops

SCHOOL DINNERS BY IAN DIGESTION

Smelly Socks by Guy O. Logical-Hazard

UPSET STOMACH by Belle E. Ache

USED BANDAGE BY E. LASTOPLAST

SMELLY STUFF

What is the favourite
game of Chinese skunks?
Ping Pong.

How does a
skunk cry?
Poo hoo!

What is a skunk's
favourite perfume?
Odour Cologne.

WHAT'S
SMELLY AND
HAS A —
PIN
THROUGH
IT'S NOSE?

What is the difference between a large,
hairy bear and a teacher?
One is smelly and covered in fleas, and
the other is a large, hairy bear.

'Knock, knock!'
'Who's there?'
'Phew.'
'Phew, who?'
'Oh, what a stink. I can
smell you from here.'

A SKUNK ROCKER!

'If frozen water is iced water,
what is frozen ink?'
'Iced-ink.'
'I know…but answer the
question anyway.'

How many skunks does it
take to make a great stink?
Just a phew.

RUN FOR
IT, GEORGE!
SOME OF THE
JOKES IN
THIS BOOK
STINK EVEN
MORE THAN
WE DO!

What did the skunk say when the
wind changed?
'It's all coming back to me now.'

Why do giraffes have
long necks?
Have you smelled their
feet recently?

Smelly feet? Stinky socks?

Sort them out with these amazing new

ODOUR
EATERZ

(Yes, we know odour-eating devices aren't a new idea but there has never been a more effective method than this one. Simply strap one of our hungry baby crocodiles to each foot and we guarantee any suspicious smells will be eaten up. As will your foot. And, anyhow, it will be hard for people to complain about your odour when they haven't any noses left.)

Who says education

standards have dropped?

Anyone who's spent a day at

Crude Street Comprehensive

knows they couldn't get any

lower than this.

Get ready to read why...

School Rules

1. No running in the corridors

(If your nose is running, wipe it on your sleeve like the rest of us do.)

2. Pupils must shower before coming to school

(Whether you decide to take that shower before the winter term or the summer term is up to you.)

3. Pupils must not pick their noses

(Noses will be allocated by teachers on a first-come, first-served basis.)

4. Pupils must not make stinky smells in the science lab

(Unless you already had a stinky smell before you went into the science lab, of course.)

THIS BOOK IS A BLOT ON THE WORLD OF LITERATURE!

5. Pupils must not complain about school dinners

(Obviously if you're still complaining, then you're still alive...which proves you didn't eat your school dinner.)

6. Pupils must not write graffiti on school walls

(There is only space for teachers to write graffiti on school walls.)

7. Pupils must have labels on all school uniforms

(This year's most popular label is 'toxic waste: do not touch'.)

8. Pupils must keep the playground tidy

(Bring all your rubbish into the classroom, where it belongs.)

9. Remember that school opens every morning at 9 a.m.

(And closes as soon as the health and safety officers come round.)

YUK IDOLS

WHO WILL BE TOP OF THE PLOPS?

NO9: D.K. DENTURE

FAVOURITE FOOD: TOOTH PASTRIES

FAVOURITE SONG: ANYTHING PLAYED IN CLUBS. (I ONLY COME OUT AT NIGHT.)

FAVOURITE SINGER: BLUES SINGERS (THEY'RE ALWAYS DOWN IN THE MOUTH!)

STOP!

THE SOCIETY FOR TIDINESS, INNOCENCE, NICENESS AND KINDNESS (OR S.T.I.N.K. FOR SHORT) HAS INSISTED ON A BREAK FROM ALL THIS YUCKINESS! SO WE'VE ASKED TV GARDENER CHARLENE BIN-NOCK TO GIVE US THE FIRST LOOK AT HER BEAUTIFUL NEW FLOWER GARDEN!

Around the House

Why were the flies
playing football in
the saucer?
They were practising
for the cup.

How do you keep flies
out of the kitchen?
Put a pile of manure in
your living room.

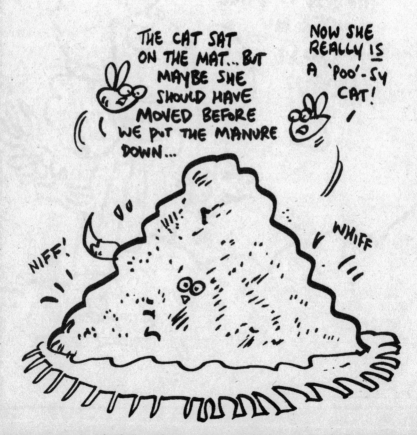

What did the slug say as he slipped down the wall?
'How slime flies.'

I THINK I'LL STAY IN HERE TILL THE BOOK'S OVER. THE CONTENTS ARE LESS DISGUSTING THAN SOME OF THE JOKES ON THESE PAGES!

WHEELIE BIN

How do you know if your kitchen floor is dirty?
The slugs leave a trail on the floor that reads 'clean me'.

What do you get if you cross a Persian rug with an elephant?
A huge pile in the living room.

WHY SCRATCH A LIVING WHEN YOU CAN MAKE BIG MONEY IF YOU USE YOUR HEAD?

NIFTY NITS™
PORTABLE NIT CIRCUS

SO YOU THINK THE SCHOOL NIT NURSE IS THERE TO KEEP YOUR HEAD CLEAN? HUH! MORE LIKELY SHE'S AIMING TO CLEAN UP HERSELF WITH THIS FULLY FUNCTIONAL 'FLEA CIRCUS' STYLE NIT WONDERLAND! TRAIN YOUR NITS TO DO ALL KINDS OF AMAZING TRICKS. DEATH DEFYING STUNTS AND **HAIR'S BREADTH** ESCAPES OUR SPECIALITY! *

*P.S. IF YOU DON'T MAKE A FORTUNE, DON'T COME LOOKING FOR US. THE FRAUD SQUAD ARE ALREADY COMBING THE AREA!

YUK IDOLS

WHO WILL BE TOP OF THE PLOPS?

NO 10: S'COOL DINNER

FAVOURITE FOOD: FOOD? WHAT'S THAT?

FAVOURITE SONG: NONE. CAN'T SING WITH MY MOUTH FULL.

FAVOURITE SINGER:
CLIFF ELVIS MADONNA JAGGER
(LIKE ME, THE NAME'S HARD TO SWALLOW.)

Bogie Belters

Mum: Are you picking
your nose and eating it?
Child: Well, you did tell me
to eat my greens.

What do bogies do
when they're sad?
Nothing – they just
green and bear it.

WHAT'S A
BOGIE'S
FAVOURITE
ICE CREAM?

A NOSE
CONE!

WHERE DO ELEPHANTS WIPE THEIR BOGIES?

ANYWHERE THEY LIKE... WHO'S GOING TO ARGUE WITH AN ELEPHANT?

What do you do
when your nose goes
on strike?
Picket.

Where do you find
bogies wearing trainers?
In a runny nose.

What did one bogie say to the other bogie?
'You're really getting up my nose.'

DOCTOR, DO PEOPLE WITH TURNED-UP NOSES GET BOGIES?

YES... BUT 'SNOUT TO BE ASHAMED OF!

What's green and scary and only comes out at night?
The Bogie Man.

Who's the number-one bogie
fortune teller?
Nostril-damus.

WHAT SWINGS OUT OF YOUR NOSE AND RINGS A BELL?

THE HUNCHBACK OF NOSTRIL-DAME!

What sweets do
bogies like best?
Pick-'n'-mix.

Where do bogies go
on holiday?
Greenland.

HOW DO YOU MAKE
AN ELEPHANT
SNEEZE?

SAME WAY —
YOU'D MAKE ITS
TOES, LEGS
AND ANKLES.

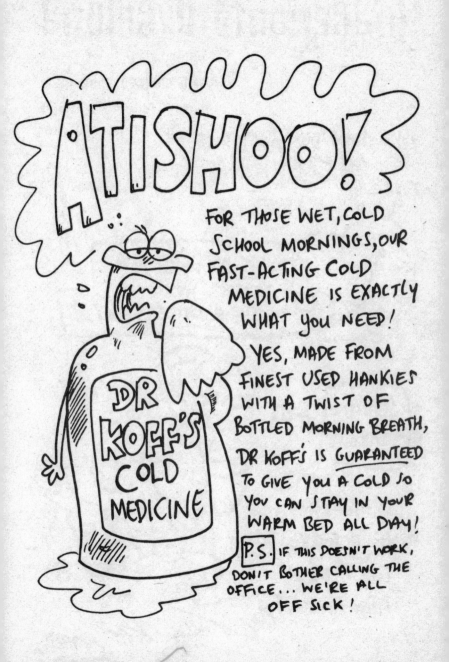

Underpants Overload

Why did the underpants have to retake their exams? They got very low skid marks.

Why does your teacher have holes in his underpants? How else could he get his legs through?

WHAT DO DEEP SEA DIVERS HAVE IN THEIR UNDERPANTS?

SQUID MARKS!

Why did the underpants jump
in the washing machine?
They wanted to go for a spin.

What's hairy, dangerous and
runs around in its knickers?
An under-wearwolf.

What's in This Old Man's
underwear drawer?
His knick-knack-paddy-pants.

Why were the X-Men chilly?
They'd lost their Y-fronts.

What do you call two
criminals in their underpants?
A pair of knickers.

What do you call underpants
that only eat greens?
Wedgie-tarians.

DO YOUR UNDERPANTS SHRINK WHEN YOU WASH THEM?

NO - PEOPLE USUALLY SHRINK FROM MY UNDERPANTS BEFORE I WASH THEM!

Sock It To Me

What did the old sock say when his hole was stitched up?
'Darn it!'

What did one old sock say to the other old sock?
'There's only a phew of us left.'

WHAT'S A VEGETARIAN SOCK'S FAVOURITE FOOD?

How do you chase a smelly
old sock away?
Shout 'Shoe!'

How do smelly old socks
hang their pictures up?
With toenails.

TOE-FU!

What do smelly old socks
dance to?
Sole music.

What do smelly old socks plug
their toasters into?
Smelly old sockets.

Why do old socks hate washing powder?
It keeps them on their toes.

What do old socks eat for breakfast?
Corn flakes.

STINK YOU VERY MUCH FOR PLOPPING BY...

IF YOU ENJOYED THE JOKES IN THIS BOOK, WHAT A STRANGE PERSON YOU ARE! IF YOU CAN THINK OF EVEN YUCKIER JOKES FOR OUR NEXT EDITION, DON'T SEND THEM TO US, STICK THEM IN THE DUSTBIN WHERE THEY BELONG.